ON BROADWAY SONGBOOK

15 BROADWAY FAVORITES

TABLE OF CONTENTS

ALMOST LIKE BEING IN LOVE Brigadoon 3

ANOTHER OP'NIN, ANOTHER SHOW Kiss Me, Kate 7

BUT NOT FOR ME Girl Crazy 13

THE COLORS OF MY LIFE Barnum 19

EVERYBODY SAYS DON'T Anyone Can Whistle 23

HEY THERE The Pajama Game 31

I COULD WRITE A BOOK Pal Joey 35

I GOT RHYTHM Girl Crazy 41

I ONLY HAVE EYES FOR YOU 42nd Street 47

LOOK AROUND The Will Rogers Follies 53

MAKE THEM HEAR YOU Ragtime 57

SEND IN THE CLOWNS A Little Night Music 63

STARTING HERE, STARTING NOW Starting Here, Starting Now 69

TRY TO REMEMBER The Fantasticks 73

WITH YOU Pippin 71

Alfred

ISBN 10: 0-7390-4386-2
ISBN 13: 978-0-7390-4386-8

Alan Jay Lerner & Frederick Loewe

It is virtually impossible to consider influential or successful writing teams without acknowledging collaborators Lerner and Loewe. Their 20-year partnership produced some of the most enduring scores ever to appear on the Broadway stage.

Born in 1918, Alan Jay Lerner was musically gifted at an early age. He learned to play the piano when he was very young and, as the son of a wealthy Manhattan businessman, he was frequently exposed to musical theatre. After attending the Julliard School of Music, he enrolled at Harvard, where he contributed lyrics and sketches to "Hasty Pudding" revues. He graduated in 1939 and became a writer for radio programs.

Frederick Loewe was born in Berlin in 1904. Growing up in a musical family (his father was a lead tenor with the Viennese operetta) inspired Frederick to become a concert pianist in his teens. In 1924, Loewe decided to move to America to pursue a career in music; he was initially able to find work as a pianist in New York, but in the years that followed, he was employed in an eclectic series of jobs, ranging from busboy to boxer. His first opportunity to write for Broadway arrived in 1938 when he was hired to write music for an operetta, *Great Lady*, but the production closed after only 20 performances.

Four years later, Loewe was in search of a librettist and having seen Lerner's work, approached Lerner with a proposal to collaborate on *Life of the Party*. The show was not a success, other than establishing the two men as a team. Their next two shows, *What's Up?* and *The Day Before Spring* were also unsuccessful, but in 1947, their fortunes changed when *Brigadoon* premiered on Broadway. With this show, Lerner and Loewe created songs and dialogue that truly defined characters. Their next hit, *Paint Your Wagon*, which depicted America during the Gold Rush, appeared in 1951 and then Lerner and Loewe spent the next five years adapting George Bernard Shaw's *Pygmalion*. The result was the classic *My Fair Lady*, one of the biggest successes in Broadway history. With its colorful characters and memorable score, *My Fair Lady* was both musically and dramatically impeccable. Their final collaboration, *Camelot*, opened in December 1960 and ran for 900 performances. After parting ways, Frederick Loewe chose to retire, but Alan Lerner found new writing partners, including Richard Rodgers.

Brigadoon

Opened on 3/13/1947
Ran for 581 performances

Tommy Albright and Jeff Douglas, two American tourists from New York, are hiking in the highlands of Scotland when they discover Brigadoon. Appearing in the mist, Brigadoon is a quaint little village with a big secret—it comes to life only once every 100 years. Upon meeting the townsfolk, Tommy quickly falls for Fiona MacLaren, even though he is engaged to be married to a young woman in New York. Fiona shares Tommy's feelings, but the schoolmaster, Mr. Lundie, unhappily informs him that their idyllic town of Brigadoon also carries a curse that prevents anyone from leaving; should someone leave, the town will never appear again. Nevertheless, a young man named Harry, despondent over his unrequited love for a local girl, attempts to leave Brigadoon, but is accidentally killed by Jeff. Meanwhile, Tommy struggles with his desire for a life with Fiona and his unwillingness to awaken only once a century. Jeff, who is sardonic and indifferent to the customs and charm of Brigadoon, convinces Tommy to return to New York. Tommy attempts to resume his normal life, but is consumed by his memory of Fiona. Hoping to again find Brigadoon, he returns to where the town appeared but sees nothing there. His overwhelming love for Fiona ultimately brings Brigadoon to life once more and Tommy chooses to live with her forever.

Almost Like Being In Love

Shortly after meeting her, Tommy is accompanying Fiona as she gathers heather for her sister's wedding. They begin to have feelings for one another almost instantly. After returning to the village, Fiona is whisked away to help her sister get ready for the wedding and Tommy is left alone with Jeff for a moment. When Jeff questions why Tommy seems so happy, Tommy sings of his feelings for Fiona in "Almost Like Being in Love."

1. ALMOST LIKE BEING IN LOVE

from *Brigadoon*

Lyrics by
ALAN JAY LERNER

Music by
FREDERICK LOEWE

Lyrics:

May-be the sun gave me the pow'r, but I could swim Loch Lo-mond and be home in half an hour. May-be the air gave me the drive for I'm all a-glow and a-live. What a day this has been! What a rare mood I'm in! Why, it's

SHORT TRACK #16

Cole Porter

Without doubt, Cole Porter is a legend in popular musical history. His astounding ability to combine unforgettable melodies with lyrics that are witty, sophisticated, clever, and often unabashedly romantic has been practically unmatched.

Porter was born in 1891 in Peru, Indiana, and grew up comfortably affluent. He displayed an interest in music early; with plenty of support from his mother, he was able to exhibit his talent by performing and writing. Primarily due to the influence of his grandfather, Porter attended Yale (where he composed two enduring football fight songs) and Harvard Law School. He showed little interest in law, so the dean convinced him to transfer to the music school. While at Harvard, he completed his first musical score along with T. Lawrason Riggs, a classmate. The show was titled *See America First* and ran on Broadway for a mere 15 performances.

Porter spent the next years in Europe, where he met his future wife, Linda Lee Thomas, a wealthy divorcee who sustained the cosmopolitan lifestyle he had become accustomed to. Although he had contributed some songs to revues and follies during the 20s, he began having modest success writing for Broadway musicals in 1928 with *Paris, Fifty Million Frenchmen, The New Yorkers*, and *Gay Divorce*. It was *Anything Goes*, which opened on November 21, 1934, that proved to be his first resounding achievement as a composer for the theatre. The show became Porter's longest running and a true classic of musical comedy.

Tragically, misfortune struck in 1937 – both of Porter's legs were crushed when a horse he was riding threw him and then fell on him. The accident severely damaged his legs and although he submitted to numerous painful operations, his right leg was amputated in 1958. Throughout these years, Porter continued to write and in 1948, he agreed to collaborate on a musical called *Kiss Me, Kate*. Replete with masterful Cole Porter songs, the show is widely considered his finest work. Two more shows, *Can-Can* and *Silk Stockings* were produced before his death in 1964.

It is a testament to Cole Porter's genius that his songs are perennial classics, still being performed and recorded by contemporary singers to this day.

Kiss Me, Kate

Opened on 12/30/1948
Ran for 1,077 performances

At Ford's Theatre in Baltimore in 1948, a theatrical touring company is presenting a musical version of Shakespeare's *The Taming of the Shrew*. The director, Fred Graham, is also starring as Petruchio and his ex-wife, Lilli Vanessi, is playing Katherine. Though divorced, and often at odds, they secretly conceal feelings for each other. Lilli is initially delighted when she receives flowers from Fred but she becomes enraged when she discovers that they were intended for Lois, the ingénue of the show. Further complicating matters, an actor in the troupe has forged Fred's signature on an I.O.U. for a $10,000 gambling debt, which two thugs have arrived to collect. The backstage antics begin to affect the onstage performance, prompting Lilli to phone her wealthy fiancé to come take her away. To salvage the performance, Fred convinces the thugs that he can only pay the debt if the show goes on. The thugs' solution: force Lilli to perform the show at gunpoint. Lilli tries to explain this to her fiancé when he arrives, but he is skeptical, partly because Fred has previously suggested to him that Lilli is impetuous. After becoming actors in the show, the thugs phone their boss about Fred's I.O.U. Unexpectedly, they find that their boss is no longer "available" and the debt is erased. The show does go on, however, and ends with Lilli's decision to stay. Much like Katherine, she realizes that she has been tamed after all.

Another Op'nin', Another Show

The cast and crew finish rehearsing the curtain call and then watch as Lilli storms from the stage in anger. Fred gives an encouraging spiel and then rushes off to placate Lilli. Led by Hattie, Lilli's maid, the cast and crew express the anticipation, excitement, and for some, routine of an opening night in "Another Op'nin', Another Show."

2. ANOTHER OP'NIN', ANOTHER SHOW

from *Kiss Me, Kate*

Music and Lyrics by
COLE PORTER

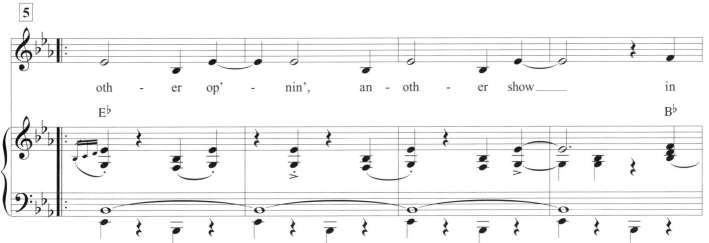

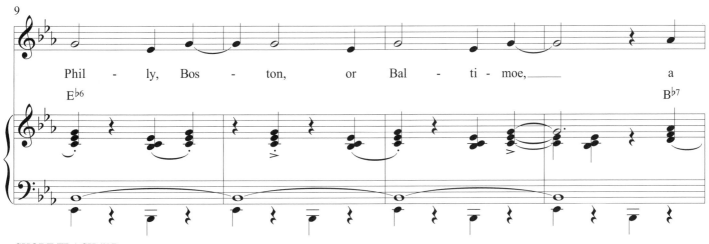

SHORT TRACK #17

George & Ira Gershwin

Widely regarded as one of the greatest composers in American history, George Gershwin was a master of styles that ranged from popular music to classical music. Much of his success, though, can be attributed to the Broadway musicals that he wrote with his older brother, Ira.

George and Ira Gershwin, born in 1898 and 1896 respectively, were the oldest of four children of Russian immigrants and grew up in Manhattan and Brooklyn. At an early age, George exhibited a propensity for playing the piano. His mother purchased a piano, intending it to be for Ira, but it was George who began formal lessons. George's passion for music was so fervent that he dropped out of high school at age 15 and went to work for a publisher in Tin Pan Alley. It was during this period that he began writing his own songs, but ironically had difficulty getting them published. George then became a vaudeville accompanist and rehearsal pianist and when two of his songs were performed at a concert, he gained the attention of a prominent publisher who offered him a job as a staff composer. At the same time, Ira began dabbling in lyric writing, using the pseudonym Arthur Francis.

After several years of songwriting that resulted in little recognition, George hit it big in 1919 with both "Swanee," a hugely popular song he co-wrote with Irving Caesar, and *La La Lucille*, a musical for which he contributed the entire score. These successes led to his commission to provide the songs for *George White's Scandals*, a series of revues that required him to compose songs in a wide array of styles. Two tremendous milestones in his career occurred in 1924: the premieres of the symphonic concert piece *Rhapsody in Blue*, and *Lady, Be Good!*, a Broadway musical comedy. *Lady, Be Good!* became the first hit for George and Ira as collaborators and began their historic legacy as writing partners. As a team, they produced fourteen Broadway musicals, from the frothy *Oh, Kay!* and *Girl Crazy* to the politically satirical *Of Thee I Sing* and *Let 'Em Eat Cake*. Written in a style reminiscent of Gilbert and Sullivan, *Of Thee I Sing* became the first-ever musical to win the prestigious Pulitzer Prize for drama; Ira shared the award with the librettists, but George was not included because he wrote the music, which was not considered a literary contribution.

Perhaps the triumph of the Gershwins remains *Porgy and Bess*, an operatic adaptation of a novel by DuBose Heyward. Distinctly American, it was the last score George wrote for the Broadway stage before his unexpected death in 1937. Several years after George's death, Ira resumed writing lyrics with other famed composers (such as Jerome Kern and Kurt Weill) until his retirement in 1960.

Girl Crazy

Opened on 10/14/1930
Ran for 272 performances

The second of the Gershwin's Broadway hits, *Girl Crazy* typifies the blithe, carefree tone of their earliest shows. It tells the story of a wealthy Manhattan playboy, Danny Churchill, who is sent by his father to a ranch in the Arizona desert. His father believes a change of environment will "rescue" Danny from the temptations of booze and women. But almost immediately, Danny transforms the place into a dude ranch complete with a dance hall, bar, gambling parlor, and girls imported from New York. The local postmistress, Molly Gray, catches Danny's eye, but rejects his advances. Danny's romantic rival from New York, Sam Mason, arrives and woos Molly; she agrees to travel to Mexico with him, but it is Danny for whom she pines. While at the hotel in Mexico, Sam's unsavory intentions are exposed and Molly returns to Arizona with Danny. As the curtain falls, Danny proposes to Molly, who has declared her love for him.

But Not For Me

Shortly after arriving in Mexico with Sam, Molly discovers Danny charming another woman. When Molly attempts to talk to him alone, Danny shows no interest and leaves her. Molly warily declares her feelings for Danny in "But Not For Me".

8

3. BUT NOT FOR ME

from *Girl Crazy*

Music and Lyrics by
GEORGE GERSHWIN
and **IRA GERSHWIN**

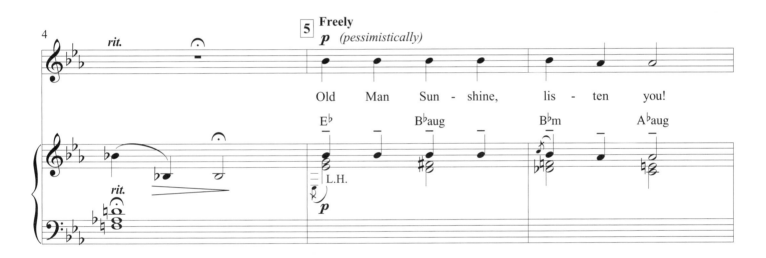

Old Man Sun - shine, lis - ten you!

Nev - er tell me, "Dreams come true!" Just try it

SHORT TRACK #18

14

* CHANGE GENDER AS NEEDED (he to she, his to her, he's to she's, he'll to she'll, feller to lady).

Cy Coleman & Michael Stewart

Cy Coleman was born in the Bronx in 1929 and by the age of six, was playing the piano in venues such as Steinway Hall and Town Hall. Because he excelled as a musician, he was able to attend the High School of Music and Art and the New York College of Music concurrently. His career as a nightclub performer began immediately after he finished his education. He formed a trio that played clubs in New York City, which gave him both steady work and recognition.

Many of Coleman's early offerings as a composer were the result of his work on various television and radio programs between 1950 and 1957. He also enjoyed success as a popular songwriter, having some of his songs performed by several notable crooners of the 50s. Carolyn Leigh became his first Broadway lyricist after Coleman made a casual offer to collaborate; the result was the 1960 show *Wildcat*, which produced the classic "Hey, Look Me Over." Two years later, Coleman and Leigh debuted the second (and last) of their works together, *Little Me*. With a new lyricist, Marshall Fields, Coleman wrote the hit *Sweet Charity*. Over ten years later, Coleman partnered with Michael Stewart and produced two musicals, *I Love My Wife* and *Barnum*, both of which ran on Broadway for over two years. A master of musical styles, Coleman continued to compose memorable theatre scores (including *The Will Rogers Follies*, *The Life*, and *City of Angels*) until his death in 2004.

Michael Stewart, also born in 1929, is among the most successful book writers ever. Prior to his work with Cy Coleman, he created sketches for *Shoestring Revue* and *The Littlest Revue* and wrote for Sid Caesar's television show from 1955 to 1959. He had an auspicious debut with his first musical libretto, *Bye Bye Birdie*. The next year, he wrote *Carnival!* and in 1964 *Hello, Dolly!* which firmly established his talents. After his collaboration with Coleman, Stewart wrote the book to the long-running *42nd Street*, and the very short-running *Bring Back Birdie* and *Harrigan 'n Hart*.

Barnum

Opened on 4/30/1980
Ran for 854 performances

In *Barnum*, the colorful life of P. T. Barnum is told through a series of scenes and songs that highlight the remarkable odyssey he made to the legendary circus center ring. Embracing the philosophy that "there's a sucker born every minute," Barnum zealously formulates one moneymaking scheme after another. His quest for the next big thing produces an eclectic variety of attractions: Joice Heth, billed as the oldest woman in the world and George Washington's nurse; Tom Thumb, the smallest man in the world; Jumbo, the giant elephant; the American Museum, a collection of oddities; and Jenny Lind, an opera singer known as the Swedish Nightingale. Ultimately, it's the "Greatest Show on Earth," (the three-ring circus), that brings him his renown.

Designed to simulate the razzle-dazzle of a circus, *Barnum* showcases jugglers, acrobats, and tightrope walkers. At its core, the show is as much about the relationship between Barnum and his wife, Chairy, as it is about the circus. Through all of his highs and lows, Barnum is guided, supported, and comforted by her steadfast devotion. When she dies, Barnum is forced to accept the truth – he couldn't have done it without her.

The Colors of My Life

Although she supports Barnum in each of his ventures, Chairy longs for a more traditional life. She suggests to her husband that he forgo being a showman and instead accept a job with a clockmaker. Barnum objects to such a routine humdrum prospect, and in "The Colors of My Life" he sings of the vivid colors he dreams of and desires to show the world. After he leaves the stage, Chairy reflects on the colors of her life, which are much more subdued.

4. THE COLORS OF MY LIFE

from *Barnum*

Lyrics by
MICHAEL STEWART

Music by
CY COLEMAN

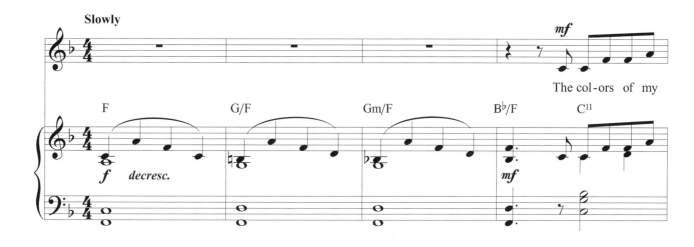

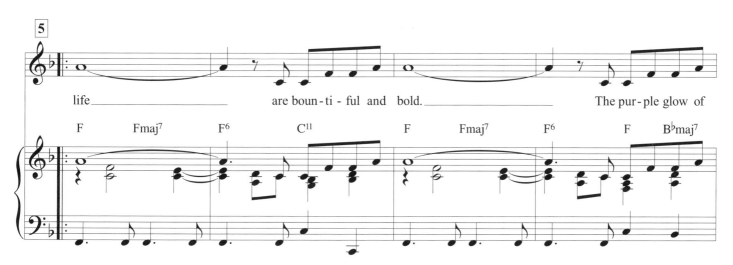

SHORT TRACK #19

20

Stephen Sondheim

Few composers of American musical theatre have stimulated as much debate, analysis, and respect as Stephen Sondheim. Musicals by Sondheim have alternately been labeled genius or perplexing, passionate or aloof. Without question, however, Stephen Sondheim has left an indelible imprint on the history of Broadway.

Born in 1930 to affluent parents who later divorced, Sondheim seemed destined for a career in theatre. As a child, he found a mentor in the legendary Oscar Hammerstein II, a family friend. Hammerstein personally guided his young protégé through every aspect of songwriting, from the development of a character and dramatic themes to the structure of a musical play. Sondheim also formally studied music at Williams College in Massachusetts, graduating in 1949 with high honors.

Years later, it was Hammerstein who convinced Sondheim to accept his first major Broadway job: writing the lyrics for *West Side Story*. Like many composers, Sondheim did not consider himself solely a lyricist (he intended to write *both* lyrics and music), but he accepted the work nevertheless. Of course, the show was a huge success and with it came his next significant lyric-writing assignment, *Gypsy*, starring Ethel Merman. When *A Funny Thing Happened on the Way to the Forum* was produced on Broadway in 1962, it became the first production for which Stephen Sondheim was credited as both composer and lyricist. Since then, he has written a wealth of shows that have firmly established his renown, including *Company, Sweeney Todd, Into the Woods, Assassins*, and the Pulitzer Prize-winning *Sunday in the Park with George*.

Sondheim's passion for puzzles is evident in his complex musical themes and his intricately constructed rhyme schemes. Throughout his career, Sondheim has been charged with creating music that is not subsequently "hummable" to theatergoers. True, Sondheim's music does not always adhere to traditional musical theatre constructs; instead, it is uniquely his own.

Anyone Can Whistle
Opened on 4/4/1964
Ran for 9 performances

The town of Hooperville, run by the unpopular mayor Cora Hoover Hooper, is going bankrupt. To save the town, Cora and her council devise a fake miracle – water running from a stone. Tourists flock to the town to partake of the well, but so do Fay Apple and her 49 patients from the local mental institution known as "The Cookie Jar." Unattended, all of the patients (the "Cookies") blend into the crowd of tourists and locals, which mortifies the mayor and her council. Curiously, Dr. J. Bowden Hapgood arrives and separates the "Cookies" from the "sane" people, but no one truly knows which group is which. Fay falls in love with Dr. Hapgood, who has become a local hero. Fearing their phony miracle will be exposed, Cora and the council devise a plan to destroy the miracle and blame it all on Hapgood. Events then become chaotic. Dr. Hapgood reveals that he's not a really a doctor, Fay discovers that the miracle was fabricated, the real Cookies are corralled when Cora regains control, and a new "miracle" is found in another town. In spite of it all, Fay realizes that she belongs with Dr. Hapgood.

Everybody Says Don't

Hapgood tries to persuade Fay to tear up the patients' records, but as usual, she is naturally reluctant and cries out "Don't!" Hapgood responds with "Everybody Says Don't," hoping she'll learn to let go of her inhibitions and conquer her fears.

5. EVERYBODY SAYS DON'T

from *Anyone Can Whistle*

Music and Lyrics by
STEPHEN SONDHEIM

better than not start - ing at all! Ev-'ry-bod-y says no, ev-'ry-bod-y says

stop, ev-'ry-bod-y says must-n't rock the boat, must-n't touch a thing!

Ev-'ry-bod-y says don't, ev-'ry-bod-y says wait, ev-'ry-bod-y says can't fight Cit - y

Hall, can't__ up - set the cart, can't__ laugh at the King!__

Richard Adler & Jerry Ross

One of the most successful, yet short-lived, collaborations in Broadway history was that of Richard Adler and Jerry Ross. Together, they wrote just two musicals – both hits that continue to be popular on stages everywhere.

Richard Adler was born in New York City in 1921. His father was a teacher and pianist, but Adler's interest was in writing. He attended the University of North Carolina to study playwriting and after he was graduated, served in the Navy for three years during World War II. It was during his brief career in the corporate world that he began songwriting. To become a songwriter in earnest, Adler left his job, but met with little success.

Jerry Ross was born in 1926 to Russian immigrant parents, also in New York. Growing up, he was featured in the Yiddish theatre as a singer and actor, becoming known as "The Boy Star," and in his teens began writing songs. He pursued his musical talents at New York University and then in the Catskill Mountains, but, although singer Eddie Fisher introduced him to music publishers, he could not make a name for himself as a songwriter.

Adler and Ross's fortunes changed when they met each other in 1950 and became a team, both adept at writing words and music. Several years later, in 1953, they produced their first hit song, "Rags to Riches," while working for music publisher Frank Loesser. In that same year, they had their first Broadway job – contributing songs to the revue *John Murray Anderson's Almanac*. They gained the attention of George Abbott, a prominent theatrical director and librettist, who chose them to write the score for a musical based on the novel *7½ Cents*. The musical, *The Pajama Game*, opened in 1954 and became a resounding hit. Based on the success of their first effort, they returned the next year to write *Damn Yankees*, again with Abbott. The result was another Broadway homerun. Much like that of their contemporaries, Adler and Ross's skill for writing commercially appealing music in a variety of styles further expanded the scope of traditional Broadway scores. Sadly, their collaborative partnership ended too soon with the untimely death of Jerry Ross in 1955. Richard Adler continued to write, devoting his considerable talent to television and concert works, for which he has received several Pulitzer Prize nominations.

The Pajama Game

Opened on 5/13/1954
Ran for 1,063 performances

The Sleep-Tite Pajama Factory has a new superintendent, Sid Sorokin, who is adjusting not only to production issues but also to life in a new town. His situation takes an agreeable turn when he meets and promptly falls in love with Babe Williams. However, Babe is a member of the local union's Grievance Committee, and when there is a dispute over a 7½-cent wage increase, the lovers find themselves on opposite sides of the issue. Babe is unwilling to budge, so Sid resorts to drastic measures – stealing a look at the factory president's company ledgers. Discovering that the president has been unethically funneling the amount of the wage increase into company profits, Sid exposes the truth, secures the raise for the union, and of course, wins back Babe's affections.

Hey There

Even though Babe is reluctant to begin a romance with a member of management, Sid has become completely captivated by her. In "Hey There," he sits alone in his office, reflecting on his feelings as he sings a memo to himself on his Dictaphone.

6. HEY THERE

from *The Pajama Game*

Music and Lyrics by
RICHARD ADLER
and **JERRY ROSS**

SHORT TRACK #20

Richard Rodgers & Lorenz Hart

With a partnership that spanned 20 years, Richard Rodgers and Lorenz Hart were one of the most prolific and groundbreaking teams in musical theatre history. They shared a philosophy that musical comedies could be mature and sophisticated, and that the songs should be an integral aspect of the story and character development.

As a child, Richard Rodgers was surrounded by music. He was born near Long Island, NY, in 1902 and at a very early age, he began to play the piano like his mother. He also began attending the theatre and developed a passion for it. He particularly idolized the composer Jerome Kern. Rodgers' parents were supportive of his love for music, so he continued to frequent concerts and operas and started to compose songs himself. In 1917, he made his debut when his older brother arranged for him to write the score for a NY boys club amateur production called *One Minute Please*. It was just one year later, at age 16, that Rodgers met Lorenz Hart.

Born in 1895 in New York City, Lorenz Hart also grew up attending the theatre. Educated entirely in private schools as a child, Hart entered Columbia College in 1913 and eventually enrolled in the school of journalism. While there, he gained some of his first genuine writing experience as the author of lyrics and skits for the famous annual Varsity Show. He left Columbia in 1917 without a degree and spent his summers putting on shows at a camp for boys.

When Rodgers and Hart met in 1918, they each recognized the other's talent and instantly knew that they would become writing partners. One year later, their song "Any Old Place with You" appeared in a Broadway show called *A Lonely Romeo*. Rodgers enrolled at Columbia in 1919. During Rodgers' freshman year, he and Hart gained further recognition for writing the Varsity Show, *Fly With Me*, and for contributing seven songs to the Broadway show *The Poor Little Ritz Girl*. Rodgers attended Columbia for just two years, transferring to the Institute of Musical Art in 1922 to study music formally for the following two years. Rodgers and Hart continued to write, but by 1925, they had only achieved minor success. They did not have the luxury of being selective, so their early work was predominately for amateur groups and benefits. Dismayed, Rodgers was about to abandon his writing career and accept a job at a children's underwear company when he and Hart were hired to write the score for *The Garrick Gaieties*. The show was a success, extending its initial run of two performances to 211 performances. Furthermore, it launched an astonishing series of Rodgers and Hart hits on Broadway that lasted until 1941, including *On Your Toes, The Boys from Syracuse, Babes in Arms*, and *Pal Joey*.

As collaborators, their working relationship became increasingly more burdensome and laborious; Hart was fraught with personal problems. In 1942, Hart's condition worsened and he encouraged Rodgers to begin looking for a new writing partner. Rodgers found one, of course, in Oscar Hammerstein II. Lorenz Hart's last endeavor with Richard Rodgers was a revival of one of their shows, *A Connecticut Yankee*, in 1943. He died five days after the show opened, ending the creative partnership of two writers who continually challenged themselves to revolutionize traditional musical theatre.

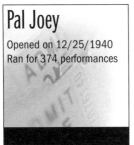

Pal Joey

Opened on 12/25/1940
Ran for 374 performances

Joey Evans is an amoral, not-very-bright nightclub entertainer in 1930s Chicago who lands an M.C. job at "Mike's Club." He arrogantly romances many of the club's chorus girls (and also a plain working class girl, Linda English), but it is eventually a wealthy older socialite who snares him. The woman, Vera Simpson, promises Joey a nightclub of his own; Joey becomes her kept man in return. As Joey and Vera prepare to open "Chez Joey," one of the dancers and her unsavory cohort hatch a plan to blackmail Vera and set up Joey to take a fall. Linda overhears the plan and warns Vera, who calls the police. The blackmail scheme is foiled, but Vera realizes that she is done with Joey. She cuts him off financially and sends him packing, leaving him right where he started – down, but not out.

I Could Write a Book

Shortly after landing the gig at "Mike's Club," Joey meets Linda on the street. She is gazing at a puppy in the window of a pet store. Instinctively, he begins weaving phony tales of his unfortunate experiences growing up and Linda is drawn in. Wooing her further, he sings "I Could Write a Book."

7. I COULD WRITE A BOOK

from *Pal Joey*

Lyrics by
LORENZ HART

Music by
RICHARD RODGERS

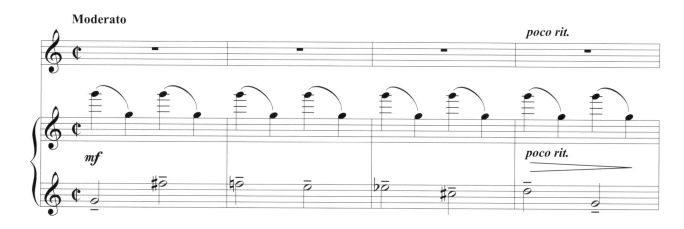

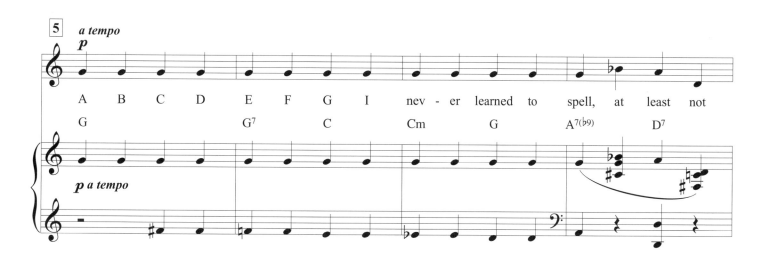

SHORT TRACK #21

George & Ira Gershwin

Widely regarded as one of the greatest composers in American history, George Gershwin was a master of styles that ranged from popular music to classical music. Much of his success, though, can be attributed to the Broadway musicals that he wrote with his older brother, Ira.

George and Ira Gershwin, born in 1898 and 1896 respectively, were the oldest of four children of Russian immigrants and grew up in Manhattan and Brooklyn. At an early age, George exhibited a propensity for playing the piano. His mother purchased a piano, intending it to be for Ira, but it was George who began formal lessons. George's passion for music was so fervent that he dropped out of high school at age 15 and went to work for a publisher in Tin Pan Alley. It was during this period that he began writing his own songs, but ironically had difficulty getting them published. George then became a vaudeville accompanist and rehearsal pianist and when two of his songs were performed at a concert, he gained the attention of a prominent publisher who offered him a job as a staff composer. At the same time, Ira began dabbling in lyric writing, using the pseudonym Arthur Francis.

After several years of songwriting that resulted in little recognition, George hit it big in 1919 with both "Swanee," a hugely popular song he co-wrote with Irving Caesar, and *La La Lucille*, a musical for which he contributed the entire score. These successes led to his commission to provide the songs for *George White's Scandals*, a series of revues that required him to compose songs in a wide array of styles. Two tremendous milestones in his career occurred in 1924: the premieres of the symphonic concert piece *Rhapsody in Blue* and *Lady, Be Good!*, a Broadway musical comedy. *Lady, Be Good!* became the first hit for George and Ira as collaborators and began their historic legacy as writing partners. As a team, they produced fourteen Broadway musicals, from the frothy *Oh, Kay!* and *Girl Crazy* to the politically satirical *Of Thee I Sing* and *Let 'Em Eat Cake*. Written in a style reminiscent of Gilbert and Sullivan, *Of Thee I Sing* became the first-ever musical to win the prestigious Pulitzer Prize for drama; Ira shared the award with the librettists, but George was not included because he wrote the music, which was not considered a literary contribution.

Perhaps the triumph of the Gershwins remains *Porgy and Bess*, an operatic adaptation of a novel by DuBose Heyward. Distinctly American, it was the last score George wrote for the Broadway stage before his unexpected death in 1937. Several years after George's death, Ira resumed writing lyrics with other famed composers (such as Jerome Kern and Kurt Weill) until his retirement in 1960.

Girl Crazy

Opened on 10/14/1930
Ran for 272 performances

The second of the Gershwin's Broadway hits, *Girl Crazy* typifies the blithe, carefree tone of their earliest shows. It tells the story of a wealthy Manhattan playboy, Danny Churchill, who is sent by his father to a ranch in the Arizona desert. His father believes a change of environment will "rescue" Danny from the temptations of booze and women. But almost immediately, Danny transforms the place into a dude ranch, complete with a dance hall, bar, gambling parlor, and girls imported from New York. Seeking jobs, Kate and Slick Fothergill arrive from San Francisco and soon Frisco Kate (a role that instantly made Ethel Merman a Broadway star) is delighting the patrons by performing in the barroom. What follows is a series of comical antics that includes mistaken identities, romantic rivalries, a cab driver sheriff, and hypnotism – all climaxing in a true musical comedy finale: the boy gets the girl.

I Got Rhythm

Kate discovers her husband Slick flirting with another young lady. She admonishes him for fawning over other women, but he sweet talks his way out of it. In "I Got Rhythm," Kate assures herself that, indeed, she has her man and anything else she could want.

8. I GOT RHYTHM

from *Girl Crazy*

Music and Lyrics by
GEORGE GERSHWIN
and **IRA GERSHWIN**

SHORT TRACK #22

Harry Warren & Al Dubin

Harry Warren was born in 1893 as Salvatore Guaragna. His parents were Italian immigrants, living in Brooklyn, NY. Without any formal training, Warren taught himself to play the accordion, piano, and drums as a child. He did not complete high school, choosing instead to play drums in a band. After a diverse series of jobs, he ended up playing the piano at Vitagraph Movie Studios. After serving in the Navy during World War I, he began composing music; his songs did not get published, but they did help him obtain a job as a song promoter with a music publishing company. He continued composing, however, and in 1922 he had his first published song. Now collaborating with a variety of lyricists, he had a string of hits in the following years, and by 1930, he was in Hollywood writing for motion pictures.

Al Dubin was born in Zurich, Switzerland in 1891 and grew up in Philadelphia. Although his parents wanted him to pursue a medical career, he had a problematic education and was expelled from both high school and medical school. Instead, he tried his hand at composing, but had minimal success. After serving in World War I, he went to Hollywood in the late 1920s. He began providing scores for musical films and in 1929, had his most successful – *Gold Diggers of Broadway*. It was in 1933 that Warren and Dubin were hired to write the score for the film *42nd Street*. The film, with Warren and Dubin's songs showcased in lavish Busby Berkley production numbers, was a hit and revitalized the movie musical genre. For the next several years, they composed solely for movies, often for more than one per year. Warren and Dubin songs were performed by many of the most popular singers and bandleaders of the era.

By 1938, their partnership ended, partly because of Dubin's personal problems. Harry Warren was no less prolific, however. Collaborating with many of the best lyricists, he continued to produce hit after hit. Al Dubin also found new writing partners and contributed lyrics until his death in 1945. Warren enjoyed three more decades of success as a songwriter, largely because of his ability to adapt to the musical trends of the times. Remarkably, almost 50 years after he wrote for the film *42nd Street*, it was adapted into a stage musical and became an astonishing hit on Broadway, running for more than eight years. Warren was able to behold the updated *42nd Street* before his death in 1981. With such a legacy of songs to their credit, Harry Warren and Al Dubin were each justifiably inducted into the Songwriters Hall of Fame.

42nd Street

Opened on 8/25/1980
Ran for 3,486 performances

New York City, the 1930s. Like many before her, Peggy Sawyer arrives with dreams of becoming a Broadway star. Almost immediately, she receives her first rejection when she discovers that she's too late for an audition with director Julian Marsh. On her way out of the theatre, she realizes that she has forgotten her purse, so she returns and ends up befriending a writer for the show, Maggie. Peggy joins Maggie and three chorus girls for lunch, where they teach her some dance steps. When Marsh sees her dance, he agrees to hire her for the show even though he doesn't need another dancing girl. Marsh has plenty of other problems to deal with, though. Because he's in financial trouble, he has accepted $100,000 from Abner Dillon, the boyfriend of the show's star, Dorothy Brock. Dorothy, on the other hand, is clearly dissatisfied with her part in the show and has secretly taken up with another boyfriend, Pat. When she tells Abner about Pat, he threatens to withdraw his financial support of the show. The chorus members rally and convince him to reconsider. The curtain finally goes up in Philadelphia, but on opening night, Peggy accidentally bumps into Dorothy, causing Dorothy to fall and injure her leg. After he fires Peggy, Marsh announces that he will have to close the show. Again the chorus members come to the rescue, not only convincing Marsh to continue the show, but also to give Peggy the lead role, now that Dorothy is out. As Peggy is about to get on a train back to Allentown, Marsh offers her the role. Peggy accepts and when the show opens on Broadway, it's a big hit.

I Only Have Eyes for You

When Julian Marsh discovers that Dorothy is secretly seeing Pat, he has a thug persuade Pat to get out of town. In Philadelphia, Dorothy announces to Abner that she's through with him and plans to reunite with Pat. Marsh again calls his thug, but Peggy overhears and rushes to warn Pat. When Dorothy discovers Pat with Peggy, she misunderstands their relationship and throws them out of her room. Alone, Dorothy realizes that she's truly in love with Pat and sings "I Only Have Eyes for You."

The song "I Only Have Eyes for You" is one of several that were added to *42nd Street* when it was revived on Broadway in 2001. The revival ran for more than three and a half years (1,524 performances).

9. I ONLY HAVE EYES FOR YOU

from *42nd Street*

Lyrics by
AL DUBIN

Music by
HARRY WARREN

SHORT TRACK #23

Cy Coleman, Betty Comden & Adolph Green

Cy Coleman was born in the Bronx in 1929 and by the age of six, was playing the piano in venues such as Steinway Hall and Town Hall. Because he excelled as a musician, he was able to attend the High School of Music and Art and the New York College of Music concurrently. His career as a nightclub performer began immediately after he finished his education. He formed a trio that played clubs in New York City, which gave him both steady work and recognition.

Many of Coleman's early offerings as a composer were the result of his work on various television and radio programs between 1950 and 1957. He also enjoyed success as a popular songwriter, having some of his songs performed by several notable crooners of the 50s. Carolyn Leigh became his first Broadway lyricist after Coleman made a casual offer to collaborate; the result was the 1960 show *Wildcat*, which produced the classic "Hey, Look Me Over." Two years later, Coleman and Leigh debuted the second (and last) of their works together, *Little Me*. With a new lyricist, Marshall Fields, Coleman wrote the hit *Sweet Charity*. Over ten years later, Coleman partnered with Michael Stewart and produced two musicals, *I Love My Wife* and *Barnum*, both of which ran on Broadway for over two years. In 1978, he had the first of two hits with Betty Comden and Adolph Green, the farce *On the Twentieth Century*. The three reteamed in 1991 to write *The Will Rogers Follies*. A master of musical styles, Coleman continued to compose memorable theatre scores (including *The Life* and *City of Angels*) until his death in 2004.

Betty Comden and Adolph Green were both born in 1915 in New York City. Sharing a fervent desire to be entertainers, they met while simultaneously searching for acting agents and performing opportunities. Comden, the daughter of a lawyer and a teacher, was a drama student at NYU. Green, a son of Hungarian immigrants, worked as a Wall Street runner while trying to find work as a character actor. Their fortuitous meeting led to a life-long creative partnership, one of the longest in Broadway history. Their initial venture together was a comedy troupe called The Revuers. Because they could not afford to hire anyone, they wrote all of their own material. The Revuers was having varying degrees of success in New York City venues when young composer Leonard Bernstein approached them in a supper club and the trio became a writing team. With the support of famed director George Abbott, in 1944 they authored the musical *On the Town*, which became a hit and established glowing recognition for Comden and Green as writers. Their initial glory was short-lived, however, and after several failed productions with other composers, they relocated to Hollywood and wrote for movie musicals, including *Singin' in the Rain*. After two years, they returned to New York City, teamed with Bernstein and produced another hit, *Wonderful Town*. At this time, composer Jule Styne suggested that they work with him; they agreed and began a team that would work together for more than ten years. Comden and Green wrote two of their most successful shows, *On the Twentieth Century* and *The Will Rogers Follies* with Cy Coleman. Comden and Green appeared on stage again in 1977, performing songs from their shows and movies. The two continued their writing partnership until the time of Adolph Green's death in 2002.

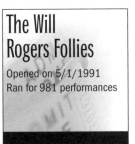

The Will Rogers Follies

Opened on 5/1/1991
Ran for 981 performances

The Ziegfeld Follies seems an unlikely setting to find a cowboy, but in *The Will Rogers Follies*, the colorful history of legendary entertainer Will Rogers is as spectacularly presented as was anything in the heyday of Mr. Ziegfeld himself. In fact, Florenz Ziegfeld (as an omnipresent voice only) guides much of the action on stage during the show. Surrounded by dancing showgirls, lassoing cowboys, and performing dogs, Will Rogers narrates his own life story. Rousing production numbers showcase the highlights of his professional career, from his start in wild west shows to his candidacy for U. S. President and his fame on the silver screen. His personal life is recounted as well. In tender moments with his devoted wife and children and in poignant songs and monologues, Mr. Rogers reflects on his philosophies, foremost among them – "I never met a man I didn't like."

Look Around

Will Rogers had a passion for the land. In "Look Around," a musical monologue, he somberly reflects on the condition of the land that he loves.

10. LOOK AROUND

from *The Will Rogers Follies*

Lyrics by
BETTY COMDEN *and* **ADOLPH GREEN**

Music by
CY COLEMAN

Lynn Ahrens & Stephen Flaherty

Born in New York in 1948, lyricist Lynn Ahrens did not initially pursue a career in musical theatre. After she received a degree in journalism from Syracuse University, she spent several years in the advertising industry. During this time, she experienced success as a contributing songwriter to the classic *Schoolhouse Rock!* animated children's series. Ahrens formed her own production company in 1978 and created a series of educational programs for children, which garnered her both recognition and awards. Four years later, she auditioned for a BMI Musical Theatre Workshop, which brought her together with her future writing partner, Stephen Flaherty.

Unlike Ahrens, Stephen Flaherty grew up participating in music. Born in 1960 in Pittsburgh, he developed an ardent interest in musical theatre and began composing as a teenager. Following his graduation from the Cincinnati College-Conservatory of Music in 1982, he moved to New York City. Because his mentor, Lehman Engel, was a founder and director of the BMI Workshop, Flaherty enrolled. There he met Lynn Ahrens and they began collaborating in 1983, with Ahrens as lyricist and Flaherty writing the music.

Their first effort, which was performed only in a workshop setting, gained the attention of a director from Playwrights Horizons; by 1988, *Lucky Stiff* premiered. A musical farce based on the book *The Man Who Broke the Bank at Monte Carlo*, the show closed after six weeks. Their next musical, *Once On This Island* met with greater success. Also based on a novel (Rosa Guy's *My Love, My Love*), the show had at its center an emotional story that dealt with love and social classes. It moved to Broadway and earned Ahrens and Flaherty significant recognition as a writing team. Although *My Favorite Year* in 1992 was a failure at the box office, their reputation was unaffected and along with ten other writing teams, they were selected to submit four songs for consideration for a new show called *Ragtime*. Ahrens and Flaherty completed the songs in less than two weeks and were selected to write the entire score. Hollywood also took notice, and the pair was chosen to write songs for an animated film, *Anastasia*. Since 2000, their Broadway and Off-Broadway offerings have been as stylistically diverse as *Suessical, A Man of No Importance*, and *Dessa Rose*.

Ragtime

Opened on 1/18/1998
Ran for 834 performances

Based on the novel by E. L. Doctorow, *Ragtime* weaves the stories of three American families at the turn of the 20th century. In 1902, everything in New Rochelle seems perfect for Mother, Father, and Mother's Younger Brother. While Father is away on an exploring expedition, Mother finds a newborn baby abandoned in her garden. The baby's mother, Sarah, is discovered and the compassion Mother feels for the young woman's plight compels her to take Sarah and the baby into her home. The baby's father is an African-American musician, Coalhouse Walker, Jr. He persistently courts Sarah despite her unwillingness to speak to him. Meanwhile, a Jewish immigrant from Latvia, Tateh, arrives in America with his young daughter and struggles to make a good life for her. Throughout *Ragtime*, these fictional characters intertwine with historical figures such as Emma Goldman, Harry Houdini, Henry Ford, and J. P. Morgan.

The era is rapidly changing and so too are the characters. Mother gradually realizes that she is much more than an acquiescent wife, Tateh perseveres through tribulations to become a successful moviemaker, and a series of tragic events leads Coalhouse into a life of radical rebellion. The remarkable and at times heartbreaking journey that the characters take is beautifully realized in great part through the songs, a kaleidoscope of early American styles.

Make Them Hear You

Demanding justice for his suffering, Coalhouse Walker, Jr. and his supporters barricade themselves inside the J. P. Morgan Library in New York City. With the assistance of Younger Brother, who is familiar with explosives, they threaten to blow up the library unless Coalhouse's demands are met. Father arrives and advises the authorities that Coalhouse will listen to only one man – Booker T. Washington. Washington enters the library and attempts to convince Coalhouse to surrender for the sake of his young son. Coalhouse concedes with the compromise that his men will go free in exchange for a hostage – Father. Coalhouse's supporters, including Younger Brother, are loyal and refuse to leave, so Coalhouse rallies them to carry on with their cause in "Make Them Hear You."

11. MAKE THEM HEAR YOU
from *Ragtime*

Lyrics by
LYNN AHRENS

Music by
STEPHEN FLAHERTY

60

Stephen Sondheim

Few composers of American musical theatre have stimulated as much debate, analysis, and respect as Stephen Sondheim. Musicals by Sondheim have alternately been labeled genius or perplexing, passionate or aloof. Without question, however, Stephen Sondheim has left an indelible imprint on the history of Broadway.

Born in 1930 to affluent parents who later divorced, Sondheim seemed destined for a career in theatre. As a child, he found a mentor in the legendary Oscar Hammerstein II, a family friend. Hammerstein personally guided his young protégé through every aspect of songwriting, from the development of a character and dramatic themes to the structure of a musical play. Sondheim also formally studied music at Williams College in Massachusetts, graduating in 1949 with high honors.

Years later, it was Hammerstein who convinced Sondheim to accept his first major Broadway job: writing the lyrics for *West Side Story*. Like many composers, Sondheim did not consider himself solely a lyricist (he intended to write *both* lyrics and music), but he accepted the work nevertheless. Of course, the show was a huge success and with it came his next significant lyric-writing assignment, *Gypsy* starring Ethel Merman. When *A Funny Thing Happened on the Way to the Forum* was produced on Broadway in 1962, it became the first production for which Stephen Sondheim was credited as both composer and lyricist. Since then, he has written a wealth of shows that have firmly established his renown, including *Company, Sweeney Todd, Into the Woods, Assassins*, and the Pulitzer Prize-winning *Sunday in the Park with George*.

Sondheim's passion for puzzles is evident in his complex musical themes and his intricately constructed rhyme schemes. Throughout his career, Sondheim has been charged with creating music that is not subsequently "hummable" to theatergoers. True, Sondheim's music does not always adhere to traditional musical theatre constructs; instead, it is uniquely his own.

A Little Night Music
Opened on 2/25/1973
Ran for 601 performances

A Little Night Music concerns the romantic entanglements of several couples as they gather for a weekend at a country estate in Sweden. Primary among them are Fredrik Egerman, a middle-aged lawyer, his much younger wife, Anne, and his son Henrik, who is secretly in love with Anne. The weekend's hostess, Desirée Armfeldt, is a theatre actress with whom Fredrick once had an affair. Desirée invites him for the weekend after the two have had a brief reunion in her dressing room, even though she is having an affair with a married count, Carl-Magnus. Desirée intends to seduce Fredrick and continue their romance. The planned seduction fails because Fredrick maintains that he is devoted to Anne. By the end of the show, Anne has stolen away with Henrik, Carl has returned to his wife, and Fredrik, realizing that Anne is gone, chooses Desirée.

Send in the Clowns

Desirée successfully lures Fredrick to her bedroom and confesses her desire to rekindle their lost romance and begin a new life together. Fredrick, a faithful husband, rejects Desirée's advances and returns to his wife. Left alone, Desirée reflects on the ridiculousness of the situation, singing the contemplative "Send in the Clowns." In masterful Sondheim style, the metaphoric lyrics appropriately parallel her career in the theatre.

12. SEND IN THE CLOWNS

from *A Little Night Music*

Music and Lyrics by
STEPHEN SONDHEIM

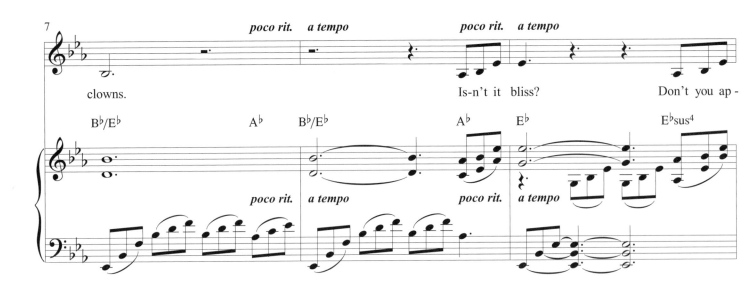

clowns.   Just when I'd stopped   o-pen-ing doors,   fin-al-ly

know-ing the one that I want-ed was   yours.   Mak-ing my

en-trance a - gain with my u - su - al   flair,   sure of my

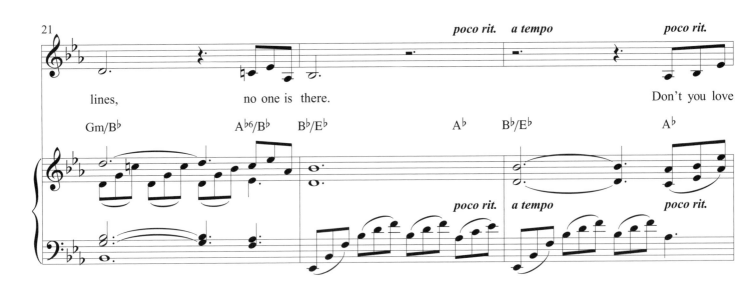

clowns?
clowns?

Quick, send in the clowns.
There ought to be

Don't both- er, they're

here.

Is - n't it

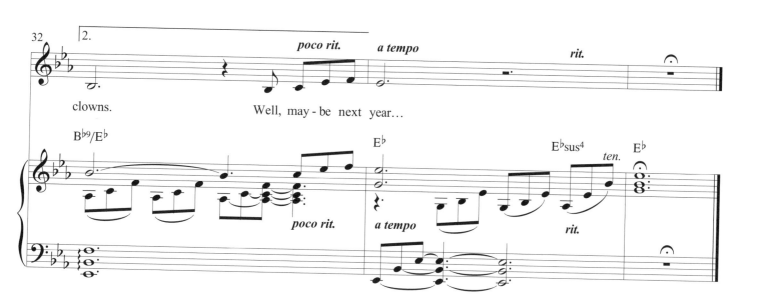

clowns.

Well, may - be next year...

Richard Maltby, Jr. & David Shire

Even before they met as students at Yale University, Richard Maltby, Jr. and David Shire had much in common – both were born in 1937 to bandleader fathers and grew up surrounded by music. At Yale in the mid-1950s, they became a writing team and their first effort, *Cyrano de Bergerac*, was staged in 1958. Shire, a piano player, composed the music, and Maltby became the lyricist. Maltby and Shire began their professional career in 1961 when they contributed songs to *The Sap of Life*, an Off-Broadway musical revue. They followed with *Love Match* and *How Do You Do, I Love You*. Throughout much of the 60s they collaborated frequently, but much of their work was produced Off-Broadway or not at all. However, several of their songs, including "Autumn" and "Starting Here, Starting Now" were recorded on albums by Barbra Streisand. While still maintaining a writing partnership, Maltby and Shire also pursued career opportunities independently of one another. Shire began composing for television programs and movies such as *Saturday Night Fever* and *Norma Rae*, while Maltby began directing for the theatre. In 1977, Maltby directed an Off-Broadway production of his material with Shire called *Starting Here, Starting Now*, and on Broadway in 1978, he conceived and directed the highly successful and exuberant tribute to the music of Fats Waller, *Ain't Misbehavin'*.

The musical *Baby*, which opened in 1983, became the first show written entirely by Maltby and Shire to open on Broadway, and in 1996 they returned with *Big*. In between, they collaborated on the revue *Closer Than Ever* and Maltby contributed the lyrics to the hit musical *Miss Saigon*. Maltby conceived and directed another big hit in 1999, *Fosse*, a compilation of Bob Fosse production numbers.

Starting Here, Starting Now

Opened on 6/19/1977
Ran for 120 performances

Starting Here, Starting Now is a showcase of songs by Maltby and Shire that comment on the many stages of romantic relationships, both good and bad. Only one man and two women appear on stage, but each song reveals a new character. A melancholy woman laments a love lost in autumn. A man emphatically declares that he's forgotten all about a failed love affair. A high-strung woman struggles to complete a crossword puzzle while contemplating her relationship with her boyfriend. Presented minimally, each musical number tells a story. In this revue, the sophisticated songs take center stage.

Starting Here, Starting Now

With perhaps some of the most traditionally romantic lyrics in the score, the title song "Starting Here, Starting Now" expresses the joy at the advent of a life-long relationship.

13. STARTING HERE, STARTING NOW

from *Starting Here, Starting Now*

Lyrics by
RICHARD MALTBY, JR.

Music by
DAVID SHIRE

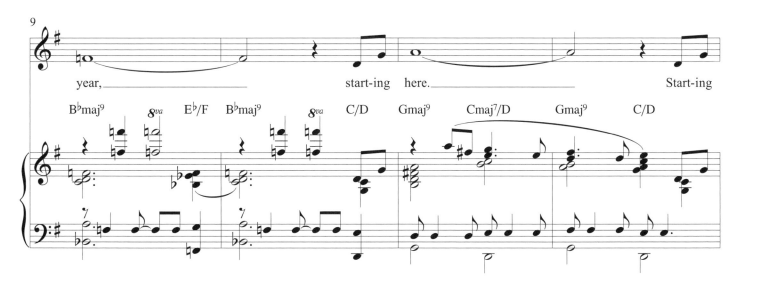

Tom Jones & Harvey Schmidt

The team of Harvey Schmidt and Tom Jones strived for simplicity in musical theatre, and together created one of the biggest hits in stage history, *The Fantasticks.*

Each born in the late 1920s in Texas, neither Schmidt nor Jones desired to be writers. As a child, Schmidt loved the music that he heard on the radio and learned to compose and play the piano by ear. Jones grew up loving to perform, although he never saw any theatre in his small town. They eventually met as students at the University of Texas; Jones was studying to be a stage director and Schmidt was an art major. Their association began when Schmidt became an accompanist for drama students in The Curtain Club, a campus theatre group that Jones was writing for. One of their earliest collaborations was *Time Staggers On*, a musical revue. After college, both men entered the Army and, wishing to continue their writing partnership, they communicated by mail. When discharged from the Army, they each relocated to New York City; Schmidt became a successful commercial artist and Jones taught some classes, but he had difficulty securing directing jobs without an established reputation.

It was in 1959 that a college acquaintance and director, Word Baker, approached them with a promising offer: he needed a one-act musical to be performed at Barnard College. For several years, Schmidt and Jones had been working on an adaptation of *Les Romanesques*, a play by Edmond Rostand, but they had abandoned it when it seemed too difficult. Within three weeks, Schmidt and Jones rewrote the piece into a one-act musical and renamed it *The Fantasticks*. The show gained the attention of producer Lore Noto, who brought it to an Off-Broadway theatre, where it ran for more than 40 consecutive years.

In the years that followed, they had several shows produced on Broadway, including *110 in the Shade* in 1963 and *I Do! I Do!* in 1966. Schmidt and Jones also wrote and staged many small-scale productions (such as *Celebration* and *Philemon*) in their private workshop. There, they could experiment with the art form much like they had done with the creation of the longest-running show in American theatre.

The Fantasticks

Opened on 5/3/60
Ran for 17,162 performances

Matt and Luisa are a boy and a girl in love, despite the fact that a wall separates them. The wall was erected by their fathers who believe that the only way to ensure Matt and Luisa become close is to let them think that their fathers disapprove. The fathers have created a ruse that they are feuding which they are eager to end, so they devise a plan to put Luisa in danger and let Matt rescue her. They procure the assistance of El Gallo (who is the show's narrator), an old Shakespearean actor, and his Indian sidekick. The plan works perfectly and Matt and Luisa are more in love than ever.

Their bliss is fleeting, though, for they learn that their fathers have been manipulating them all along. They begin to bicker and see the imperfections in one another. Convinced that they both need to experience more of life, Matt ventures into the world and Luisa chooses to dally with El Gallo. The young lovers discover that the world without each other is wrought with disillusionment and discontent, and that they truly belong together.

Try to Remember

The narrator, El Gallo, begins and ends the show with "Try to Remember." He sings of moments in life and the memory of days gone by, of the passage of time and the changing of the seasons. When he reprises the song as the show draws to a close, the deeper meaning of his words becomes evident – just as spring arrives from winter, the heart is made stronger only after it has felt pain.

14. TRY TO REMEMBER

from *The Fantasticks*

Lyrics by
HARVEY SCHMIDT

Music by
TOM JONES

SHORT TRACK #24

17

Try to re-mem-ber the kind of Sep-tem-ber when grass was
Try to re-mem-ber when life was so ten-der that dreams were
Deep in De-cem-ber it's nice to re-mem-ber with-out a

G   G/B   C⁶   D⁷   G

22   *cresc.*   **25**   *mf*

green and grain was yel-low.___
kept be-side was your pil-low.___
hurt the heart is hol-low.___

Try to re-mem-ber the
Try to re-mem-ber when
Deep in De-cem-ber, it's

C⁶   D⁷   Bm⁷   Em⁷

cresc.   *mf*

27   *decresc.*

kind of Sep-tem-ber when you were a ten-der and cal-low
life was so ten-der that love was an em-ber a-bout to
nice to re-mem-ber the fire of Sep-tem-ber that made us

Am⁷   D⁷   Gmaj⁷   Cmaj⁷   F

decresc.

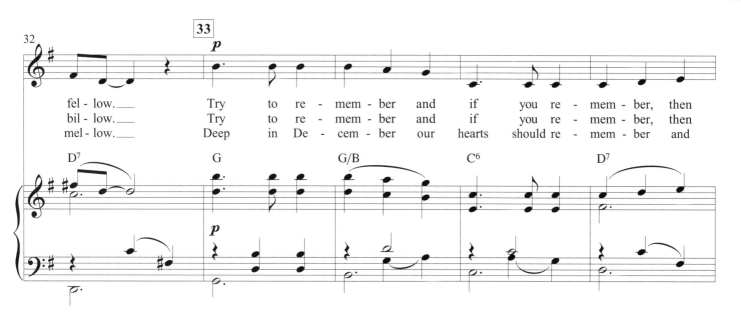

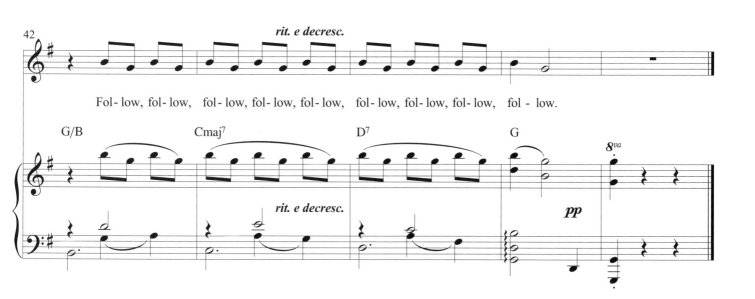

Stephen Schwartz

When musical theatre ventured in a new direction in the 1970s, fresh talents like Stephen Schwartz were at the forefront. With a combination of pop, rock, and folk musical styles, Schwartz wrote for Broadway audiences that were hungry for theatre that reflected their generation's tastes.

Stephen Schwartz was born in New York City on March 6, 1948. While still in high school, he studied piano and composition at the Juilliard School of Music and in 1968, he received a Bachelor of Fine Arts degree in drama from Carnegie Mellon University. It was during his years at Carnegie Mellon that he began to compose works designed for the stage, including a piece called "Pippin, Pippin."

Schwartz returned to his native New York and accepted a position as a producer for RCA Records. Shortly thereafter, he began working in the theatre when one of his songs was used for the play *Butterflies Are Free*. The first of his shows to be produced was the exuberant *Godspell*, based on the gospel of St. Matthew. The next year, *Pippin* opened on Broadway and became a genuine hit. When *The Magic Show* appeared two years later in 1974, Schwartz had the rare honor of three simultaneously running Broadway shows. Soon after, he directed and contributed several songs to *Working*, but then remained absent from the theatre until 1986's *Rags* (as lyricist) and *Children of Eden* in 1991.

Hollywood beckoned and Schwartz spent the next several years applying his theatrical style to animated films, with much success. During this time, he also recorded and released two collections of songs from his anthology. He made a triumphant return to Broadway in 2003 with *Wicked*, a huge success that once again showcased his knack for writing songs that hit all the right chords for a new generation of theatergoers.

Pippin
Opened on 10/23/1972
Ran for 1,944 performances

Pippin tells the story of a young man's search for complete fulfillment. The son of King Charlemagne, Pippin initially believes that he should follow in his father's footsteps and become a soldier, but the glories of war elude him. He then indulges in the pleasures of the flesh, which also proves fruitless. His stepmother, Fastrada, subtly convinces him to dethrone Charlemagne by killing him. Pippin complies, but when the peasants begin to rebel, he realizes that he is unequipped to be a ruler. Escaping to the countryside, Pippin is taken in by a young widow, Catherine, who puts him to work on her farm. Feeling trapped and still discontent, Pippin once again flees to find his "corner of the sky."

Throughout all, Pippin is beguiled by the mysterious and magical Leading Player, who eventually attempts to convince the young man that the only path to pure fulfillment is to sacrifice himself in a spectacular blaze of fire.

Pippin ultimately realizes that the perfectly extraordinary existence he seeks cannot be attained, so he shuns the Leading Player and chooses the simplicity of a life with Catherine and her son.

With You

Pippin visits his grandmother, hoping to receive some bits of insight. She regales him with examples of her carefree philosophy toward life and love. Pippin is inspired and decides that he should stop worrying and just enjoy life. His first step: discovering the beauty of romance in "With You." Each time he sings the title lyric, Pippin refers to a different nameless lover.

15. WITH YOU
from *Pippin*

Music and Lyrics by
STEPHEN SCHWARTZ

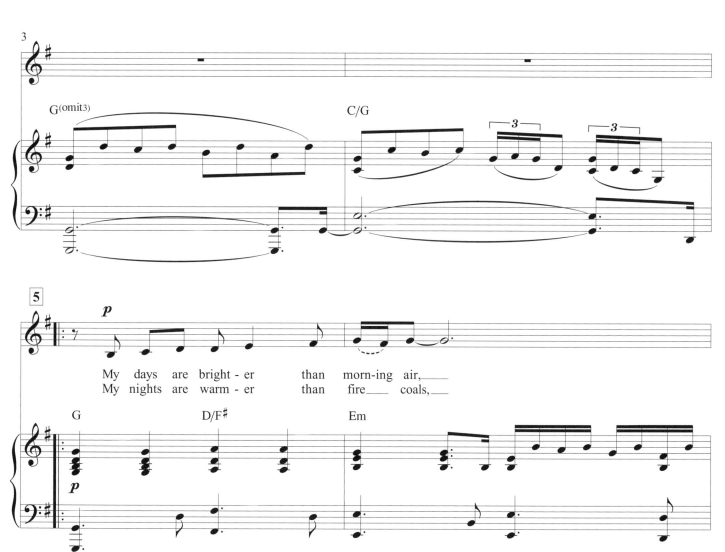

My days are bright-er than morn-ing air,_____
My nights are warm-er than fire____ coals,_____